BOOKS BY SIR WILFRED T. GRENFELL

THE ADVENTURE OF LIFE

THE
ADVENTURE OF LIFE

BEING THE

William Belden Noble Lectures

FOR 1911

BY

WILFRED THOMASON GRENFELL

M.D. (Oxon.), C.M.G.

BOSTON AND NEW YORK

HOUGHTON MIFFLIN COMPANY

The Riverside Press Cambridge

THE WILLIAM BELDEN NOBLE LECTURES

This Lectureship was constituted a perpetual foundation in Harvard University in 1898, as a memorial to the late William Belden Noble of Washington, D. C. (Harvard, 1885). The terms as revised by the founder and accepted by the President and Fellows of Harvard College, November 26, 1906, provide that the lectures shall be delivered annually, and, if convenient, in the Phillips Brooks House during the season of Advent. It is left with the Corporation to determine the number of lectures. Each lecturer shall have ample notice of his appointment, and the publication of each course of lectures is required. The purpose of the Lectureship will be further seen in the following citation from the deed of gift by which it was established : —

"The object of the founder of the Lectures is to continue the mission of William Belden Noble, whose supreme desire it was to extend the influence of Jesus as the way, the truth, and the life; to make known the meaning of the words of Jesus, 'I am come that they might have life, and that they might have it more abundantly.' In accordance with the large interpretation of the Influence of Jesus by the late Phillips Brooks, with whose religious teaching he in whose memory the Lectures are established and also the founder of the Lectures were in deep sympathy, it is intended that the scope of the Lectures shall be as wide as the highest interests of humanity. With this end in view, — the perfection of the spiritual man and the consecration by the spirit of Jesus of every department of human character, thought, and activity, — the Lectures may include philosophy, literature, art, poetry, the natural sciences, political economy, sociology, ethics, history both civil and ecclesiastical, as well as theology and the more direct interests of the religious life. Beyond a sympathy with the purpose of the Lectures, as thus defined, no restriction is placed upon the lecturer."

TO MY WIFE

PREFACE

I should like to preface these lectures which I am about to deliver by a brief foreword concerning the man in whose memory they have been founded. William Belden Noble was unknown to me personally, while probably some of you at least had the advantage of his acquaintance. I think I can truly say, however, that I am conscious of his friendship. A life like his makes him, like Kim, a friend of all the world.

He loved the things I love: football and athletic games. He was human in social relations and a member of clubs which, had I been at Harvard, I should have wished to join. He worked and played and loved — hard. His was just a strenuous, natural human life. And in addition to all this, but not in spite of it, he had the vision of the real value of life. He ranked high at college. It cannot be said that it was lack of intellectual ability which gave him the faith, which I hold is of more value than anything else on earth.

So I am fully persuaded, not only that William Belden Noble lived, but that he still lives the imperishable life of those through whom the life of God is manifested.

Those are the alumni of Harvard who will ever be among her benefactors. Have you no debt to her and to those who shall fill your places when you too shall have "passed beyond the bourne of time and place"? See that you strive to discharge your indebtedness while you can. If of the gold and silver some of you may be able to give her, there is that which has cost you both in labor and life, to you who give, that shall sweeten tenfold the joy of giving. But that which alone all of us can give, and which all of us must give if, like William Belden Noble, we are to be worthy to be remembered as her sons, is what her truest counselor, Phillips Brooks, asked of you, — the gift of yet one more regenerated human life.

WILFRED T. GRENFELL, M.D.

December, 1911.

CONTENTS

THE ADVENTURE OF LIFE

LECTURE I

LIFE AND FAITH

THE object of the Noble Lectures, as I
conceive it, is decidedly a practical one. It
is that something may be said, and in such
a way that it shall induce in the minds of
the hearers a keener desire to stand for just
those things which Christ did stand for. It
is to beget a determination to reincarnate
his life, in the conviction that so our brief
tenure of human life may be most useful,
most completely fulfill the purpose for
which it was given, and so attain the whole
achievement of which it is capable.

I cannot but realize the difficulty of the
problem presented, while at the same time
I entirely believe in the supreme importance
of it. I appreciate most deeply the honor
that I should be asked to attempt the task.

I must be enjoying much the same sensation as the diminutive Jack when he stood before the giant's gate, which is exactly my idea of the "joie de vivre."

The choice of the medical profession as a lifework should of itself be a guarantee that one looks upon human life as worth while. For it is scarcely conceivable that one should devote his entire stay on earth to the effort to discover and carry out methods for preserving and prolonging that which he considered practically valueless. Being unskilled in philosophy and theology, the method I propose to adopt in these lectures is bound to be empirical, and may possibly appear egotistic. As I do in purely professional work, so now, I can, I believe, best argue from my own experience as to what I think may be helpful to others. I recognize, however, that there are spiritual and mental variations in human minds corresponding to well-known physical differences known to medicine as idiosyncrasy, and I can only plead for indulgence if I am guilty of judging others too much by myself.

I therefore begin my first lecture by stating that I am an intense believer in life as an asset of incomparable value. I cannot remember the day when I had not a passion for life, — it seemed so full of adventure. Stimulated by trophies of Indian jungles which had been sent back by our uncles and which graced our home, I decided, almost before I learned my alphabet, that the profession of tiger-hunting was the only one worthy of the name. Indeed, all my leanings, hereditary or otherwise, were towards a life of action. My forebears have almost all been physical fighters, and I presume I could hardly have escaped the heritage of a hatred for peace and platitudes. An English public school only emphasized in my mind the conviction that physical contests were the most desirable in which to excel. It never occurred to me that the boys who labored at their books could have discovered a field for adventure. I did not for one moment think that they were worthy of anything but the general contemptuous opinion so aptly expressed in the names by which we knew them.

It was in London, when I was first on my own allowance, and free from any supervision of body or mind, that I discovered that mental activities offered a chance for adventure as real and as worthy as any physical field. There I began to appreciate the value of knowledge because it enabled one to do things. When in the operating theatre I watched men familiarly and with confidence achieving magnificent results in relieving pain, prolonging life, and restoring capacities by their masterly mental qualifications, life seemed suddenly to loom up ten times as attractive as I had ever dreamed it could be. But there was a larger realm of thought which no one could fully comprehend. Many of my teachers were men with wide reputations, who were to me almost as demigods, but among them there was a vast difference of opinion on this subject. Some were silent, all were reticent regarding it.

The ordinary exponents of the Christian faith had never succeeded in interesting me in any way, or even in making me believe that they were more than professionally concerned themselves. Religion appeared to be a profession, exceedingly conventional, and most unattractive in my estimation, — the very last I should have thought of selecting. I considered it effeminate, and should have strongly resented the imputation, and felt heartily ashamed, if any one of my companions had suggested that I was a pietist. I am not excusing my position: I am stating it. I made an exception of the home religion of my mother, which I simply put in a category by itself.

I was attracted one day by the excitement of an enormous crowd outside a tent. I was living at that time in Whitechapel, in the sordid purlieus of which the famous Jack the Ripper was contemporaneously carrying on his profession. One saw every

kind of evil, and every variety of wrecked
humanity, but among many vanquished,
some victors. The fight between good and
evil in the individual was always an evident
fact. It never occurred to me that I must
at some time, willy-nilly, enter consciously
into the same arena. I went into the tent,
and there I heard a plain common-sense
man talking in a plain intelligible way to
a huge concourse of really interested people.
The man made me feel in all he said that at
least he had thrown every ounce of himself
into the issue. In a most matter-of-fact but
kindly way, he pulled up a long-winded
prayer-bore, who was irritating the audience with droning platitudes, and the
Almighty by conferring quite unnecessary
information upon him. He even cut short
the choir and braved the organist, when
he realized that their silence helped more
than their art. He ended with an address,
the simplicity of which left no doubt in
any man's mind that he was a fighter for
the practical issues of a better and more

cheerful life on earth, a believer in a possible life of big achievement for every soul of us, both here and hereafter. His self-forgetful appeal for help left a determination in my heart at least. Perhaps I had been wrong in considering the main object of the preaching profession to be preferment rather than social uplift. It was a revelation, it opened a new vision, and I guessed for the first time the meaning in the eyes of the knights of chivalry in familiar famous pictures. Somehow religion as an insurance ticket had never interested me. The selfishness and even cowardice of that appeal, to which I had so often listened, now loomed up in the worse light of distrust. That which I had called faith was after all unfaith. The new faith which there dawned on me for the first time was not the conviction that God would forgive me, but that he had already given me things of which I had not even known; not that he would save me, but that he would use me. I went out with yet a third field for adventure before me,

and far the largest, to add to the glory and
beauty of life.

A new factor which now forced itself
upon me was my will. I believed in free
will: it seemed common sense. I knew that
materialists did not, and that most of my
comrades believed in Darwin and Huxley,
and in the teaching that we are all slaves of
unbreakable laws. I believed that I was at
the fork of two roads, and could go down
the one which I liked. For my venture I
wanted knowledge. At that time I thought
nothing of reading just as late at night as
I could stay awake with a wet towel round
my head; but I recognized limits to my
capacity. I was forced to admit that there
were some things too high for me. And yet
— I must go ahead. Only thus will any
man find his field for adventure. Courage
and every noble virtue, and every idea of
the romantic, worth-while world in which
I live would be gone, if I did not believe
in free will. "After all, it is not that we
strive to do the impossible, but that which

to the self of mere experience looks impossible." [1]

I was prejudiced for an adventurous world. The other dull material world was unbearable to me anyhow. Science taught us that the phenomena of life worked out in an orderly manner; and that from observing the facts governing that order, certain results were discernible. The embryo of an egg developed wings and flew. A similar embryonic cell in the ocean grew fins and swam. The processes never got mixed and no human being could alter them. Some men who posed as scientists (that is, those who knew) talked as if "nature" or the "laws of nature" controlled all these wonderful things. They were so familiar with them that they might almost have invented them. But the "forces of nature," the *force* that is outside ourselves thenceforth to me spelled "God." It is merely a fact that no man, however much he wishes, can really make mystery a bar to faith.

[1] Bishop Brent, *Leadership.*

All business has to be conducted to some
extent on a credit basis. The same system
applies occasionally in the realm of thought;
and I am justified in using it in the sphere
of convictions. I am convinced that this
is a case in which wisdom is justified of her
children. In Ottawa there is a statue of
Sir Galahad, erected to the memory of a
young man who, seeing two skaters fall
through the ice on the Ottawa River, sprang
in to save them and was drowned himself.
On the granite base of the statue are carved
the young knight's words, "If I save my
life I lose it." Reason may say he was a
fool, but is that wisdom? When the Lake
Erie steamer caught fire, in order to save
the passengers it became necessary to steam
full-spead ahead to the nearest beach. The
flames drove the passengers forward. Some
one must stay at the wheel to steer, or all
would be drowned or burned. The keel
struck the beach just in time. But when
they looked for the helmsman, Robert
Marsden, only a common sailor, they found

him dead, his blackened body lying sunk down on its knees in the chart-room; he himself had lashed his hands to the wheel. The Master was ridiculed as a madman; but the Greeks did not blame Achilles for his choice. Are all heroism, all impulsive nobility, all honor, because they are unreasonable, to be classed as folly, and to be sneered at?

Once in a heavy cross-loop on the Dogger Bank, the forestay of our schooner suddenly broke. While I was reasoning out what to do, the skipper had her before the wind, relieved the pressure at once, and saved the mainmast, and probably our lives. A snap judgment, an instinctive decision, is not necessarily an unreasonable one.

For my part, I came to see I must start somewhere, and stand on some basis. Should I stand on the current knowledge of the early eighties, which was about as stable as a Labrador bog and has already gone the way of flesh, or should I stand on faith? Down which road should I go? Whether demonstrably intellectually correct or not, I decided I would prefer and therefore would try to follow the Christ.

What is the explanation of the biased or even bitter spirit in which many men deal with the claim of Christianity to their attention? In medicine and in all other branches of science we are at best supposed to bring our problems to the bar of our intelligence, without a bias for proving or disproving, but simply to find the truth. I have had men come in the middle of the night, come many miles, incur considerable expense, just to discuss prolonging the life of a patient, who had no more claim on them than that he was a fellow man in distress. Their sole desire was to get wisdom for action, and they considered it a mean thing to worry one iota about the trouble involved in the attempt to prolong mortal life. The very men who strain at gnats when it is a question of real life, swallow a camel when it relates to mere animal existence.

Among other odd things which struck
one with regard to the acceptance of Christianity as a method of life was the fact that
the people to decry it most loudly as a remedy were those who had never tried it at
all. The loudest denouncers of a remedy
for the body should be those who have
tried it without prejudice and found it a
failure. It is considered unscientific and
irrational for a man to do more than remain silent about a remedy he has not tried
personally. If, however, he were to form
his opinion by watching others try it,
it would be equally unscientific to judge
of the experiment unless he were assured
it was the unadulterated remedy he was
seeing used. Those who have studied
Christ's own teachings for themselves, and
seen his varied methods tried for humanity's sins and sorrows, have never been dis-
appointed. Most of us must find God, if
at all, in the experiences of everyday life.
One cause is almost alone enough to justify
and quite sufficient to explain the attitude

of mind in which men of science approach
the Christian religion. For the claim of
priest and theologian and religious teacher
of succeeding ages, that their particular
faith was knowledge and included absolute
truth, was as demonstrably false as it was
immodest. "Truth cannot exist in a church
any more than learning can in a university." Again, their ceaseless attempts to
stereotype the intellectual and social relation of every man of all ages according
to their own conception of what the religion of Christ called for has patently held
back the true advance of the race. They
captured the title of the Christian Church,
"vi et armis," just as a knight does the
token from his adversary's helm, and ar-
rested the growth of the real church, till
it became like a miserable stunted cretin,
for whom for centuries no cure was thought
possible. Moreover, they enforced their
tenets in a way well calculated to leave
objectionable impressions on the minds
of scientists, even if they did escape the

experience of Galileo. No wonder that, as
McComb says: "People are weary of the
burden of theological doctrines, and are
asking for something permanent, something
verifiable in experience, which no criticism
can touch and no progress in culture
wither."[1] A young German divine is reported to have said, "Christ came to save us
from the theologians!" Not to be misunderstood, I would say here that I am myself a
member of a church, and comforted by the
fact that the visible church is, willy-nilly,
enlarging its views as to what it means to
be a Christian, and is ever more and more
recognizing the social side of the service of
the Master. On the other hand, with the
increase of knowledge, the arrogance of
current thought is groundless, and the
scholar no longer believes he has a monopoly of religion. As Peabody has pointed
out, the scholar has discovered that "the
conceit of learning arises from not discern-
ing the dimensions of truth"; and that "the

[1] *Christianity and the Modern Mind.*

contest between religion and science now interests only a few belated materialists and a few overslept defenders of the faith." [1] We must reach the hilltop of learning before we can hope for the full view. Emerson says, "Talent sinks with character." The Master differs from teachers like Rousseau, for there is no hiatus between his precepts and his character. Spiritual satiety has been the trouble with many scientists, just as men, after a dinner they cannot digest, are unable to climb the hill.

Besides this cause, the heritage of wrong aim, the fact of sin, the heirloom of bad advertisement also remain. To make men enter the church to-day there exists only the same road which leads to love for her Founder. After an address at the Cooper Union in New York, a rabid anti-Christian was fiercely heckling the speaker from the audience and abusing the church of to-day. His arguments were so drastic and yet so specious that there was only one way to

[1] *Religion of an Educated Man.*

answer him. "Are you a member of any
church?" the speaker asked. "What are
you getting at?" was the astonished reply
"Well, I've been for twenty-five years,"
continued the speaker, "and I assure you
it never encouraged me to rob, to kill, or
to vilify. If you really want to satisfy your
mind, I advise you to go and join the
church, and see for yourself what she
stands for." The suggestion was so novel
that the critic rose and walked out.

On returning to Labrador one spring, I
chanced to be discussing with a group of
men on the wharf the reported conversion of some of the toughest and hitherto
untouched characters among the settlers.
It happened that, like so many others, they
had been bred to despise the idea of conversion, though laboriously drilled in many
denominational doctrines of doubtful value.
That a conversion like St. Paul's, which
meant something practical, could occur
in the twentieth century, or anywhere outside the Bible, seemed to them ridiculous.

There was a lot of looking down and nervous kicking the ground when we endeavored to talk of it as one would of catching fish. They all admitted, however, that the whole cove had been altered, and men and women entirely changed for the better. Various boats with different kinds of apparatus for catching fish were coming to and fro from the company's wharf as we were talking. All were engaged in getting fish for the same firm, and all were eager enough to gain their end. The fish were not trapping well, and the humbler "hook-and-line" men were the only ones who were getting anything. I suggested that it would not be to their credit as loyal employees or as men of common sense, if the trap-net men should regard as enemies, or find fault with, or try to ridicule, their successful comrades, for using methods other than their own. The suggestion that the adoption of such a course of action could possibly be considered a fair demonstration of what Christ taught at once brought a denial to their lips, and

a side-glance as well to see if I were really
in earnest. Yet this was exactly the attitude of one body of Christians to another.
There was no rejoicing, that I could see,
that the sole purpose for which their own
organization avowedly existed was being
accomplished, but recrimination that it was
not being accomplished in their way. In
this case, however, the whole group of men
immediately indorsed the general principle that different methods were entirely
necessary in the material world, and also
that excellent results had been obtained
in this instance, for which their own sect
had nominally striven. It had certainly
failed for so long a period as to endanger
the desired result being accomplished during the lifetime of the very people who had
now become new men.

I could cite many instances where faith
in Christ has very apparently altered a
man's whole outlook and action. Naturally,
most of my observation has been among
fishermen, and it has included men of al-

most every kind of temperament. One was a man with whom I afterwards made several voyages. A man of exceptionable physique, he had been the victim of uncontrollable temper, and various of his drinking sprees had ended in the police station, as the result of violent assaults on others. He had destroyed his home and his wife had left him. He was rapidly ruining his own splendid physique, and the lives of all those with whom he came in contact. Suddenly he became sober and peaceful, built up his home again and took back his wife, and developed an absolutely unselfish passion to try to save his fellows from the slavery that had been his. He always claimed that his faith in Christ was the secret of the change. He was so cheerful and so uniformly optimistic that his very face became transparent with happiness, and I have never had a more delightful shipmate. I once asked him to say a word to encourage other men. He stood up to try, and unaccustomed tears coursed down his cheeks. At last he said, "To think of the like of me talking to them men," and sat down. This class of men has been well illustrated by Mr. Harold Begbie in his "Twice-Born Men" and "Broken Earthenware." In my own experience it has been multiplied many times. Indeed, I have often wondered why so many clergy and other workers have asked me whether I have read these books, as if the results they describe were rare experiences. It is only the recording of them that is rare. There is a reticence always on the part of all good workers to draw deductions from their own work prematurely. There can be no question of their occurrence, however, though my own experience shows me that these more emotionally susceptible men are most liable to temporary retrogression. But even so, I am devoutly thankful for such changes as may occur to change their life and environment, changes which I can attribute to nothing else but their faith. I am certain that any one who, even though without faith himself, though also without prejudice, would seek to record such cases in the way we record cures of disease, — which only affect part of men's lives, — would be surprised at the extent and value of suddenly acquired faith in the Christ.

Before leaving my seafaring friends, however, I would say that, while the suddenness of the change of habits and of life has been unquestioned, the process, it has always seemed to me, has been less brief than they themselves supposed, and the conversion could have been almost as justly attributed to many previous experiences. Yet I ought to add that the majority among these fishermen who are endowed with the kind of faith that dominates their whole life are conscious of the day on which it became a potent factor in their lives, — a most helpful experience, it always seems to me.

Among those of my own class in life, I have been privileged also to see not a few very remarkable changes; but the process has almost always been gradual, and usually accomplished through unselfish service, which is Christ-following. In men of my own profession I have seen just as unmistakably the results of Christian faith. From self-indulgent, destructive, wasted lives, I have seen them become just such ministers to humanity as I conceive that Christ calls for. Among the unfortunate victims of extreme wealth I have known some suddenly accept the Christ's view of stewardship, and without dumping their wealth, for which Christ never called, they have accepted their responsibilities, and administered it with such love and wisdom that their renewed lives have entirely stopped the mouths of critics.

I do not believe in labels, but I must accept that of utilitarian. For such an attitude faith is an absolute necessity. At the age of nineteen I was living with a clever lecturer on the "Evidences for Christianity." His shelves were literally crowded from floor to ceiling with scientific and philosophical works of every kind, ancient and modern. His life and talents were entirely devoted to demonstrating that our Christian faith was in accord with the scientific knowledge of that day. He was popular, and I believe to some extent successful in influencing men's opinions and lives. Anyhow, I have seen him carried home on the shoulders of a London crowd, and finishing his address from our upper window. At that same time my own brother, who had taken an open scholarship and a brilliant "first" in Classics at Oxford, had just finished his "greats" examination in philosophy. In this, to my infinite surprise, he had secured only a second-class. His fault, according to the examiners, was his brilliant memory. He had quoted accurately the teachings of masters at variance with one another to examiners who did not agree with any of them. "Where wise men differ, fools may come in," and I rejoiced that I felt free to decide to order my life on the basis of Christian faith, a position

I have never regretted having adopted.
Phillips Brooks says somewhere that "freedom of belief should not mean freedom to
believe little but freedom to believe much."
On a perfectly common-sense basis, I have
always trusted that when I differed from
the teachings of creeds and sects, possibly
I was as likely to be right as they, since I
had as direct access to and as great a claim
on the promises of the Giver of all wisdom
as they.

There exists an absolutely undeniable
antipathy on the part of theologian and
scientist alike to allowing this freedom.
One says you shall not have it, the other
says you cannot, though the value of its
acquisition has the indorsement of thousands, nay, millions of our fellow men of
all ages.

Yet we cannot take up a newspaper
without seeing accounts of these same men
suing others for restitution of goods or
money out of which they have foolishly
allowed themselves to be swindled.   In

these cases any judge would like to say to
them, "You'll get no redress, for it is only
what you deserve." The same applies
to matters which affect our lives more
intimately and permanently. Take, for
instance, marriage. The ever-increasing
number of divorces show how these most
vital and personal relations are undertaken
without any reference whatever to reason.
It is the same with our play: aviation,
motoring, polo, football, cards, billiards,
etc. We go into them entirely without
reference to their value to our especial
temperaments or requirements or capacities or physical interests. In food and drink
the folly and credulity of man is shown in
the absolutely unreasonable extent to which
men indulge themselves. Whatever the
result may be in the brevity or longevity of
life, these excesses affect every expression
of mind or spirit as surely as they do the
physical capacities. It is not unusual for
the famous Billy Muldoon to announce to
a new degenerate, "Sir, you have no mind.

For the next six weeks you will have the infinite advantage of Billy Muldoon's mind."

One might multiply these instances indefinitely, but the only point I wish to urge is that it is these very people who in everyday life stigmatize even the man whose life has been demonstrably benefited by the Christian faith as a fanatic, as a man of ill-balanced mind, as credulous. But so strange are the contortions of mentality that many times men have said to me, "I wish I could believe as you do; it would be such a help and such a comfort." At the same time I have known men with death threatening, and in agony of mind for those they must leave behind them, to whom I have wished above all else I could give that peace and rest which the acquisition of that faith invariably carries with it. But it has been impossible. "Christ's appeal is not *primarily* to the emotions or to the intellect, but to the will." It is not that men cannot accept the Christ nearly so much as that they will not.

One of the causes of this mistrust of the
Christian faith in men's minds is the age-
long misrepresentation of it. We have such
erroneous ideas of what the Christ pleads
for. "In that unhappy moment, centuries
ago, when the church set up a metaphys-
ical text, in place of the standard of moral
excellence and personal fellowship with
Christ, it lost its supreme distinction of
symbolizing the unity of all life in a common divine source and in a common immortal destiny." [1] Such bad advertising as
Christianity sometimes gets would certainly kill the desire even for an Eastman
kodak or a Winchester rifle. D. L. Moody
said, "The Christian is the world's Bible,
but we often need a revised version."

It was at this decisive point that for the
first time I realized I was, and puzzled as to
who I could be, and why I was, and what
I could do, and where I was bound. Some
people think the last question is mere silly
sentiment. But it really is not only most

[1] Paradise, *The Church and the Individual*, p. 248.

natural but most common sense. In passing
a vessel at sea we almost always ask first,
"Where are you bound?" Somehow that
actually interests us most. I have found
that if I know the vessel and have any
affection for the skipper I am ten times as
likely to be concerned. I never knew one
to resent my question, and his answer usually closed with "Where are you?"

Now it so happens that most of my cruis-
ing has been done in the foggiest region of
the world, and I myself have often enough
been for days together in the fog. Because
the season is short and the distance to be
covered so great, to get along is always
a question of first and imperative importance if we are in any way to satisfy ourselves that we have done our duty. It is a
horrible feeling at the end of the season to
find one has delayed and had to miss out
sections of the work. This is not because
we have to render account to any one but
ourselves, but simply because we find that
we are far less willing to condone any faults

or omissions than a master over us would
be. It therefore happens that often we have
to run ahead in spite of the fog and take
the risk. Incidentally these are among the
most exciting times of our lives. The risk
itself, the adventure, is the real spice of
what would otherwise be prosaic and dull.
Indeed the fact that the coast is badly light-
ed, poorly charted, and devoid of landmarks
and buoys on the shoals, not only keeps us
alive and quickens our capacities but gives
us a realization of fellowship with our friends
sailing the same seas. Thus we get a much
more intelligent love for one another as
we see each other's fallibility, and we come
to feel that the work is more worth while
because it involves adventure, and because
we have seen that not every man can or
will "launch out."

I must admit, however, that when running in the fog the first question on one's
lips as one sights a fellow voyager is not,
"Where are you bound?" but "Where are
we?" I remember the first time we were

crossing the Newfoundland Banks. We had spent some days in blanketing fog without a heavenly or earthly body to give us any information about our position. We were somewhat anxious, not knowing which way to go. Suddenly, a huge three-masted ship loomed up out of the fog, apparently running off her course with confidence. We had time to cut her off and ask where we were. She replied by hanging over the side a huge blackboard with the approximate latitude and longitude on it, and then disappeared into the gloom. We were not able to prove it, but we trusted her good faith and acted as if it were true. We did n't in the least resent the suggestion of interference in our private affairs. Many and many a time since I have had to rely on the opinions of others and even their gratuitous help. At one time we were running somewhat too confidently on a part of the shore which we thought we knew perfectly well. Indeed, we were running full speed in spite of our inability to see. We were

suddenly aroused in the wheel house by
the united shouting of half a dozen sten-
torian voices, "Hard a' starboard! Full
speed astern! — or you'll be ashore."
These presumptuous people in a trap
fishing-boat had, quite unasked, interfered
to make us change our course, and had
thereby saved us from a catastrophe. It was
so dense we could not see the breakers.
However, we found we had made no mis-
take in instantly acting on the faith that
they were wiser than we, without waiting
to argue the rationality of it. But beyond
this, on yet another occasion in thick
weather we ran right by a boat full of men
and almost instantly afterwards sighted
breakers. We escaped practically by a
miracle, but we felt badly that the men
in the boat had not interfered to warn
us.

These and every experience of life seem
to teach that when the question at issue
is of vital, practical importance to us we
have no prejudice against outside advice,

and that there is no reason why we should not offer such as we may possess, nor why we should not accept it and act upon it as if it were true, without needing intellectual demonstration.

Dr. Crile has shown that anger, fear, love, anxiety render protoplasm granular; just as the shaking of steel makes a much-worked axle brittle and unreliable, so these emotions destroy the cells in the cortex of the cerebral hemispheres just as would poison or a blow. It is through these important cells that the outside world is interpreted to us. So faith that brings peace, is, in any case, a physical desirability if not a moral one.

The man who has no interest in life, its meaning and its future, is only intelligible to me on one of three hypotheses: either he has never faced himself and never stopped to think, or he has done it with blind eyes and closed ears, or he is no man at all.

I can understand the position of the spectator at the great games; being unable to play himself, he certainly does his best to show his sympathy and give his support to the players. He spends much energy and at times makes a very fine show. But his outlay is more or less pathetic, for he is only a spectator after all, — and he is so numerous! I know there is no need to waste sympathy on the actual players. The glory of the game liberally compensates them for any damage they may receive. The man to whom my sympathy always goes out is the substitute, ready and anxious to get into the game — but to whom the chance is never given to use his capacities. His loyalty calls for unbounded admiration.

If there is iniquity in accepting a course for true, the axioms of which cannot be demonstrated by mathematics, this is the reason why I rejoice in my iniquity (in accepting the Christian faith). My choice has given me such fun in life, and still promises to do so. For no capacities need go unused in the field of Christian adventure.

I have as much right to my position as any man has to unfaith, — and I have the deductions of common sense to support me. As for the materialist, he at least cannot blame me. If I am all wrong, I am at worst the victim of his own inexorable system. When we recognize our finiteness, we come to faith as rational. I do not expect to see God here, and live. As Chesterton[1] has pointed out, though somewhat sweepingly, "Between Hegel who believes in nothing but himself and his senses, and the materialist who believes not at all in his senses," stands Christianity as the great Modus Vivendi.

If I were to quote in the classroom the words of the Scripture, that the natural man does not *want* the things of the spirit, I should probably be hooted at or mildly ignored, and yet it is perfectly obvious that this is really the case. Even if we know the

[1] G. K. Chesterton, *Orthodoxy.*

best path, we *wish* to walk the one that
may not cost us anything in everyday life,
rather than let reason sit master on our
control. If I were to quote Christ's saying,
"I came not to send peace, but a sword,"
the retort, even if unspoken, would un-
doubtedly be, "What did Christ know
about it?" Yet the unfailing evidence of
facts shows every day the inevitableness of
the contest if the best is to be made of life.
Life to the Christian sounds a clarion call
like the last words of Marmion: —

"Charge, Chester, charge;
On, Stanley, on."

Without question unfaith is too often a
synonym for "don't want." It is like the
farmer who, when urged to give up whiskey,
remarked, "Prove I don't like un, and
I'll give un up."

"The great causes of God and humanity
are not defeated by the hot assaults of the
Devil, but by the slow, crushing, glacier-
like mass of thousands and thousands of
indifferent nobodies. God's causes are never

destroyed by being blown up, but by being sat upon. It is not the violent and anarchical whom we have to fear in the war for human progress, but the slow, the staid, the respectable. And the danger of these lies in their real scepticism. . . . Though it would abhor articulately confessing that God does nothing, it virtually means so by refusing to share manifest opportunities of serving Him." [1]

It is not to complain weakly of prejudice, to besmirch those who do not believe as I do, that I have thus dwelt on the strange reluctances in accepting faith as a guide for action in matters which relate to our highest interest and life. Surely in the business world men take ventures without waiting for intellectual comprehension. When the venture is of such vast importance as accepting a guide for life's action, when the Christian faith has been so unanimously approved by those who have really adopted it, when there is at least a possibility that

[1] George Adam Smith, *Minor Prophets*, vol. II, p. 54.

not only our day of life here but the life in eternity will be benefited, why is it irrational to accept the mystery and stand on the ground of "Lord, I believe. Help thou mine unbelief."

LECTURE II

In my first lecture I endeavored to defend
the deductions of my own experience,
namely, that as we all must act the conscious selection of the pathway pointed out
by Christ is rational: first, because it is the
most remunerative solution of the problem; secondly, the most interesting, as
affording a sound basis for fighting, for
loving, and for hoping; thirdly, the most
manly, as involving hard work with no
immediate vision of finality; and last, because it bases the whole on the satisfactory
presumption that I am I, and choose this
course myself.

I now propose to try and indicate how
this choice works out in men's lives whatever their temperament or activity. I am
convinced that no man can truly say,
"Christ's way succeeds for the man across

the street, but not for me." I do not argue
that a man can by his will power make
himself believe this suddenly, if his education and mentality make him sceptical
of it, or that any other man can by superior wisdom convince his mind of the truth
of it by much talking. But I do contend that
with however little faith a man starts out
if he is willing to work on that faith instead
of arguing he is on a sure road to satisfy
himself of the truth of it, and eventually
to know, as far as we can know anything,
that the Master was and is perfectly right.
You cannot find the Christ by searching
with the eye in books and pamphlets;
you cannot demonstrate him to the ear in
theological lectures. I have known more
than one man try these very ways, and
lose in the process the little faith with
which he began. The way to find the truth
about the Christ is to be willing to under-
take the kind of life that common sense
translates his teachings to mean in this age.
When at Christ's bidding the paralyzed

man found that he could walk, and the palsied man that he had strength in his arm, and the blind man that he could see clearly, they were all convinced of the Master's power, — and the cleansed lepers acclaimed him before ever they went to the priests for confirmation of their cure.

The popular idea that Christ asks men to sit down in life and admire him is absurd on the face of it. The greatest Worker the world has ever known asks men to be men and follow him in the manifold directions which always commend themselves to mankind in the supreme moments of life. It is not our recognition as we pass on the road of life that he desires, but our personal loyalty; not vain oblations, but "ceasing to do evil and learning to do good." His direct appeal is to our sense for a reasonable service. It is always more the appeal of the musician than that of the dialectician. The ear hears, but the soul interprets. The musician does n't argue; he plays, and the ear that hears recognizes or interprets the

beauty of the message without being driven
into a hole by words. Alas, for the ears
to which a Beethoven sonata reveals no
beauty, or the eyes which cannot see the
glory of the solar spectrum. To me it is certainly the fault of our interpretive faculties
if we find no attraction in the person of Jesus
Christ. Just so it is sin or moral perversion
which prevents flesh and blood revealing
Christ, and that is why faith is the best
service we can render humanity.

A long and varied experience with many
of the churches has left me confident of the
wisdom of joining one or other of them.
None have a monopoly of perfection, but a
roving life has taught me that when a man
is hungry he can well afford to overlook
imperfections in the service, so long as the
food is good. One morning, after I had
been addressing a large Bible class, a keen
young fellow came to the house where I was
staying and asked for an interview. He
said: "I got an entirely new view of what
Christ really expects of me, and I realized

that that is not taught in my church. What would you advise me to do?" I told him I had had some patients who could n't assimilate food even in the form of milk, and that I should advise him to go around till he found nourishment in *some* church, and then cultivate loyalty to that; not to stay out just because it was human and imperfect, but to go in and make it better. I find that the cause of the trouble is just as often the stomach or constitution as the meals, in these days when the public also is enlarging its views of what good food is, and beginning to insist upon having it. While the Master always insisted upon faith, he had no severe rebuke for doubt. I don't believe any of us would have let Thomas off quite so easily.

Bishop Brent [1] has said: "A man's vocation is the sphere in which to illustrate his precepts"; and I now propose in a few words to try and show how the Christian faith affects my own profession.

[1] Brent, *Leadership*.

The temptations of the surgeon are not the same as those of the priest or the scholar. His special temptations are to think that the prolongation of existence limits the call of life on him, and affords a field large enough for all he can contribute; secondly, professional prejudice against lay interference.

Regarding the first point I have never doubted that the prolongation of some lives is altogether undesirable. One or two examples of this type will suffice. An old sailor captain with cancer of the throat, which woke him with horrors that some one was strangling him as soon as he dozed off to sleep, would ask me so piteously at night for a lethal draught that I used to try and tiptoe past his bed as I went round the wards to avoid the pain of having to refuse him. A poor fisherman, incurable and mentally degenerate, owing to a creeping paralysis, is here after six years, killing and starving his family, as he, an absolutely unintelligent mass of flesh and bones, lies groaning and moaning in bed. Already one married daughter has died, worn out with caring for him and her own young family as well. His wife is rapidly sinking also.

Among my patients in hospital to-day is a young man of nineteen. He has been under my care for eleven months. He has tubercular disease of the hip and spine; there is no hope of his recovery. We cannot keep him, and must instead send him home to be a source of physical danger, a ruinous expense, and a cause of untold mental anguish to his loved ones. In the cases of the criminally insane, the tubercular insane, the hopelessly insane, the sufferers in the last stages of incurable diseases, and others, it is at least open to debate if a year or more added to their life on earth is of any value. It is questionable if the same may not be said of the hopeless moral degenerate whose vice has injured him beyond possible physical recovery. The state admits this to a certain extent in the use of capital punishment, and in its methods of preventing criminal reproduction. Theologians as well as materialists have assented to a limit to the day of grace. Pathologists have demonstrated the damage caused by the neglect of these precautions on the part of the state. I am not arguing that it is possible as yet to identify the candidates for extinction, but that it is not a worthy end for our profession in any case to limit their aspirations to utility to the prolongation of mortal life. To have life is not nearly so important as to use it well. Emerson aptly asks, "What is the use of eternal life to a man who cannot use half an hour of this life well?" What we have is never so important as what we do with what we have.

The world will, I know, acquit me of egotism in claiming for the profession of healing a special capacity for influencing the whole life of the whole man, if only because of the advantages it has in getting really close to men when they are apt to be both impressionable and thoughtful, and stripped of all conventional restraint. The real end of all social service should be to build up character; "to educate personality is true religion."[1] The ideal object of the best doctors, lawyers, scholars, priests, or indeed of every good man, is in reality the same as that of the Master.

I once carried a plant I had found to our professor of botany for identification. "Young man," he said, "a botanist does not know one plant from another." Rousseau wrote a standard textbook on how to bring up children, and dropped all five of his own, on the day they were born, in the post-box of the foundling hospital. An aurist proposed the theory of the telephone, and a business man made it of service to the public. But science and utility are coming together. It was left to the young University of Kansas to risk the opprobrium of having prostituted learning to commercialism, by appointing an unlimited staff of industrial

[1] Peabody, *Religion of an Educated Man.*

"Fellows," the object of each being to discover practical values for apparently useless products. Through their special scientific knowledge they obtained casein from buttermilk, diastase from alfalfa stalks, pituitin from the hypophysis of whales. To-day the school and university and social training in England still discount all commerce and practical productive work, as less worthy of the true gentleman than either fighting, sporting, or speculating. When the first site for a hospital in Labrador was given me by a merchant, he embodied in the deed of gift that I was not to trade there, for fear of competing with his own store. I remember that the proviso jarred on me in those days as being almost an insult. Since that I have started a long series of cash stores, believing them to be the most necessary remedy for many of our diseases. But it still seems to rub the wrong way when I am asked for how much I will sell a gallon of molasses. Christ himself teaches that the effective use of learning is not purely intellectual. The awakening of the soul to the need for an alliance of the utilitarian motive with our will is one sure stepping-stone to the Christian faith. "This faith can be kept alive," said Cardinal Newman, "only by personal holiness of life." It is not irreverent to classify the intellectual concessions rendered imperative by the willingness just to be useful, or by the view of life that the object is greater than the way in which it is achieved, with those greater sacrifices of faith which induced men to go uncomplaining to physical death for others. This is far from saying that the end justifies the means. I plead only for the adoption of a concession that is as ennobling as it is invaluable.

The great risks and sacrifices that doctors have ever been willing to accept — and our profession yields to none in the long list of willing martyrs to duty, or the advancement of learning, when the value of the object in view has been demonstrated to them — is indisputable. It would indeed

ill become so humble a member as myself
to offer any criticism whatever on a profession able to claim such a record of heroic
deeds for the sake of others. I am but ven-
turing to suggest, because I love it above
all others, that it too may not yet have
mounted high enough on the hill of divine
truth to value to the full the glories of its
own opportunities.

I make this statement because I am absolutely convinced of the value of religious
faith to the bodies as well as to the souls
of men, and because the true physician
must minister to the whole man if he is to
accomplish his best work. Nor is this deduction founded upon abstract argument,
but upon concrete proof. Admitting as we
must that prevention is better than cure,
my own experience teaches me that the
Christian faith has succeeded in eliminat-
ing causes of disease by stimulating people
to adopt the provisions of preventive
medicine. It is conceded that the greater
number of bodily ailments are avoidable

and due to preventable causes; and that the real contagion that produces many diseases is evil spiritual influences, such as feeble wills, together with evil companionship and bad environment. It does not take special knowledge or apparatus to discern this fact.

Lawyers and clergy, as well as doctors, know the endless evils to which alcohol leads. True, they may not attribute directly to it the subtle sclerosis of liver and kidney and brain, the hard artery, the fat and generally degenerate body. But they see the poverty, starvation, cruelty, accidents, and injuries to which it leads. This is just as true of the sexual and social vices. They see the provisions that society makes to pander to them, the red-light districts, the ruined girls, the debased men. But they do not, as we do, see young wives most literally murdered, blighted and miserable children, and the evident results in reducing vitality, making people incapable of withstanding disease or responding to surgical help, or in producing cancer or insanity. This is no less true in the case of the other great enemy of our race, tuberculosis.

If the employers of labor were Christian men following Christ, labor would receive fairer reward, workmen would be better housed and able to provide more healthful conditions for their families. Cleanliness, ventilation, and sanitation would be made easy instead of almost impossible. It would seem that the physician might well object to the ideal Christian conditions. Surely Christ-following is my worst enemy, for there will be no room for me in a really Christian community, when tuberculosis, sclerosis, typhoid and social evils are eradicated. In the City Beautiful of the Christian vision it is said there shall be no more sickness or suffering or death. Unless the calling of the physician is a mere isolated factor, disjointedly cast into a hotch-potch of a universe without definite aims and views, this must be the ideal he wishes to

attain. If he does not believe it is ever
realizable, and yet thinks of it at all, his
only alternative is insanity.

The answer is simple. It is this that is the
glory of our profession, namely, that, working in the spirit of the Master, it must
evolve, its keynote being self-elimination.
It has cleared the Panama of yellow fever;
it has banished typhus and plague and
black death, and almost eradicated small-
pox, diphtheria, and malaria; it has broken
the back of cerebro-spinal meningitis and
sleeping sickness, and many other ills of
the flesh. The world does acclaim that the
doctor is the best missionary if only he
has the vision and follows it. I heard Sir
Frederic Treves, the famous surgeon, aptly
say, "Medicine is the best education in the
world, yet it seems the worst profession to
follow." Because, while it gives men infinite power, incomparable opportunities,
when competition from overcrowding of
the profession arises it leads to such awful
temptations. A selfish politician, lawyer,

clergyman, or merchant has not quite the same power over flesh and blood, and does not depend so directly upon other people's misfortunes for his income. But it was the Master's profession, if he had a special one, and to me it calls as loudly for men of his mind and life, with the true Christ-following faith, as ever it did, and as insistently. It still calls for men endued with the power that comes from on high, as well as with an up-to-date knowledge of surgical procedure, and fully sympathetic with the desire which made Paul say, "I am eager to tell the good news, since faith is the power by which God brings salvation."

To be more concrete for a moment, I would state that the whole stress of the modern view of medicine is that fresh air, pure food, more hours of rest, better playgrounds, and schools and garden villages are a more remunerative investment from a medical point of view than an enlarged pharmacopœia. The use of drugs seems to be falling more and more into unprofessional hands, and I doubt very much if the unqualified chemist and patent-medicine vendor are not far the firmest believers in them. Of course there are valuable drugs, and naturally the physician should know best how to handle them. But often enough he gets into a routine, and it has been said that the average doctor never uses more than a dozen different prescriptions, and those no longer contain a dozen ingredients each. I asked a world-famous surgeon the other day what he used if he sprained his own ankle. He named a well-known patent liniment; for an irritable cut or scratch he used a patent ointment; for a digestive trouble, a famous patent pill.

On the other hand, who to-day doubts the intimate correlation between health of mind and of body, or the mutual interrelation and dependency of both of these with the soul, which expresses itself through them. Take for instance the nervous instability that results from the high pressure of modern life. What an enormous

factor it forms in the category of sicknesses.
The records of every member of our profession well confirm the statement that a
large proportion among our cases consists
of neurosis, neurasthenia, nervous prostra-
tion, and so-called functional and idio-
pathic disorders dependent upon causes
the nature of which we cannot identify
under the microscope, but which we think
are due to brain-cell instability. What a
long step toward the millennial conditions
will be covered when these disturbances
can be banished.

Once in a clergyman's [1] study before
morning service I noticed on his table a pile
of unopened letters quite a foot in height.
"Why don't you open your letters?" I
asked. — "Those all came this morning,"
was the reply. — "They are all from people
wanting help or money?" — "No, mostly
for nervous disorders and such troubles." —
"I wish you would give me an example." —
"Well, here is one. This young man has

[1] Dr. Elwood Worcester, Emmanuel Church, Boston.

been to no less than three doctors, and
in one hospital, for subjective stomach
troubles. They found no cause they could
remove. We discovered he had a burden on
his mind, which he could n't get rid of. It
prevented his sleeping. We found we could
help him, and he has lost all his pains."

One day while I was attending Dr. Barker's clinic at Johns Hopkins, the first patient brought into the theatre gave much
the following history. He had had nose
trouble, went to a specialist and had his
adenoids removed; got throat trouble, and
had his tonsils out; got bladder trouble,
and had his prostate removed; got an ob-
scure pain in his abdomen, and had his
appendix out; had headaches and pain
in the eyes, went to an eye specialist and
got glasses. Altogether this was the tenth
clinic he had experienced. On entering
the very room in which we sat we had heard
the sound of the builders of an enormous
new wing to the hospital, for which millions
of dollars had been given. Dr. Barker ex-

plained to his classes, as soon as the patient
had gone out, that in all probability this
new psychiatric hospital might have saved
this unfortunate gentleman some of his
organs. It is quite an error to suppose that
specialization and limitation of a surgeon's
field always marks the advance of scientific treatment. On the contrary, in ancient
Rome there were specialists on diseases
of the eyelashes. I presume if they could
have made a living they would have
specialized on one eyelash. That a germ,
a poison, a fee; or an injury, a knife, a clean
scar, should describe the whole rôle of the
doctor, is untenable.

At the beginning of this lecture I suggested that prejudice against lay interference is as characteristic of our profession as of any other. We certainly believe,
and every now and again state, that there
is no "hinterland" containing remedial
methods of demonstrable value outside our
own field, though our asylums for the insane plainly show us that no one is so in-

conceivably certain he is right, and knows it all, as the person of unsound mind. It is lamentable but true that we have to confess this, though that is better than that we should have to learn that there is some value in the statement from outsiders like Bernard Shaw.

Recently the English papers have been full of a lawsuit against a well-known manipulator of joints and bones in London. This man, though without a professional degree, has for years, according to the evidence of his numerous patients among the rich and educated, been effecting cures of joint troubles. A patient with an incurable knee trouble who went to him endeavored subsequently to get money out of him, alleging malpractice. The hostility and generally unfair attitude of the doctors who were called in as witnesses evoked a most convincing and scathing article in a magazine, from one of the most famous of the English surgeons, enumerating cases that he had himself been unable to relieve and which had been greatly benefited when he sent them to the defendant. He clearly proved that the man knew and used methods which we ought to adopt as being superior to our own. It so happened that one of my friends in India whose polo pony fell upon him had an exactly similar experience with this very bonesetter. While I believe patent remedies as a rule are used in inverse proportion to the intelligence of the people, I claim that humility rather than arrogance is the best attribute of the physician, and that more faith in powers outside himself is justifiable and desirable. Osteopathy, Eddyism, Dowieism, faith-healing, optology, and all extreme swings of the pendulum of protest, afford evidence of the desirability of the larger view for which I am pleading. There can be no doubt of the physical value of a peaceful mind. Yet it almost cost Mesmer his reputation and his life when he suggested that mind could be made a remedy for bodily ailments. Morton, the unfortunate introducer of ether, fared even worse. Harvey, the discoverer of the circulation of the blood, met a similar fate. Lister did not escape bitter attacks when he discovered antiseptics. Whole societies have come into existence to discredit the work of men like Jenner, Pasteur, and other incomparable benefactors of our race, while no available means are to-day neglected to prevent the opportunity of acquiring new truths by experiments on animals; to minimize the value of the results achieved, or even to injure the personal reputation of those who are humane enough to endure being so greatly misunderstood in order to minister to mankind.

It cost Paul much suffering and eventually death to advocate at Rome faith in the Christ as the means of a man's salvation. The same preaching of the same Gospel, interpreted in terms of our modern view of what Christianity means, its applicability to the whole man, has, to my knowledge, cost more than one good man almost as bitter an experience of hostility in the United States of America; for I question if words do not hurt as much as stones and whips, in these days when the advance of civilization has made us "more sensitive to and more capable of suffering." The preacher of to-day is saying that not only are physical remedies called for, not only are mental suggestions needed, but that we must ourselves be channels of the higher life, through which spiritual streams from the Power above us must come forth, if we are to contribute our best service to our fellow men. In this latter point we rejoice that he is beginning to overtake George Fox, who preached the same message three hundred years ago. We must consciously reach up our trolley arm, that contact with the Power above may give us an impetus which we cannot have of ourselves.

The value of mental suggestion has been greatly impressed upon me by many cases in my own experience. The following will serve as an example. While the guest of a doctor in Montreal I was much interested by his experiments in alcoholic cases with chloride of gold, which I had always thought to be an inert drug. A whole series of cases of ordinary alcoholism and of paroxysmal dipsomania were successfully treated, many of which had defied all former efforts. One specially interesting case was that of a cook who for over forty years had been a chronic rather than a periodic drunkard. She was savagely drunk when she came to the surgery, and a better impersonation of our vague idea of the Devil I have never seen. She was immediately injected with gold chloride and told she could drink all the whiskey she liked, but that soon she would n't care for it. She came again next day and was admitted to a private ward for a few days' rest and upbuilding. She was again injected and told to go on drinking the liquor, which was actually poured out and put in a glass on the table beside her bed. She was also told not to drink it if she did n't like it, since now that she had been given the drug the liquor would make her sick. I went in to see her that evening The whiskey on the table was untouched. She made a good recovery and returned to her occupation. I not only purchased the drugs and outfit, and tried them, but sent the directions to a well-known London physician to try also; but in our hands the system failed. Some years later the Montreal doctor, who was to read a paper on the subject before the medical society there, wired me to come and testify to the authenticity of some of his cures, as he feared the society was hostile to him. He read his carefully prepared paper, and narrated case after case. Afterwards, I gave my confirmatory evidence. The president said, and the meeting indorsed the statement, that chloride of gold in their hands was as useless as water, but none of them for one moment doubted that in the hands of the author it was perfectly successful.

Recently Lord Mount Stephen gave a

large share of his immense wealth away to
his heirs and friends, that in his life he
might have the real joy of sharing it with
others.

> ". . . For if our virtues
> Did not go forth of us, 't were all alike
> As if we had them not." [1]

A doctor's joys, no more than his success,
can be estimated by the size of his fees, or
what he gets out of his profession, but only
by what he contributes to it. That "he
who will be greatest must be the servant of
all" is certainly true of this ministry. This
is surely what the lawyer and the clergyman and the doctor desire: the conversion
of the aims and efforts of the mind, the body,
and the soul. When this is realized, a man
may say, "I am a living factor in the cre-
ative purpose, and fidelity in my place is
the test of the effectiveness of the whole
design. This unity of the world saves some
men from the conceit of wisdom, as it saves
others from the despondency of work."

[1] *Measure for Measure*, I, i, 34–36.

To refer to the value of ministering to the whole man and not to connect it with the name of Dr. Richard Cabot were impossible. While approaching it from another point of view, the world is learning to look upon him as chief apostle of the need for this all-inclusive ministry.

Myers has said that when it is a question of inquiring into whether mind acts on mind without the body, savants cannot, and theologians will not, accept evidence. But while there may be much truth in satirizing many preachers as Stigginses, I am convinced that it is not the whole truth, any more than that there is no truth in the subliminal self.

To turn now to the second division of our lecture, the profession of the law. I almost fear to tread on that ground. Though acting as a magistrate for over ten years, I am obliged to confess that I have been unhampered by any special knowledge of the technicalities of the profession, and as a medical exponent I have naturally had a remedial and not a retributive bias.

Surely, the true lawyer's ideal is not a crime, a retribution, a fee, though he too is tempted to keep so close to the mill which grinds out dollars that he may lose the full vision of his potentiality. Christ as a lawyer would, exactly as if a doctor, be working for big and worthy ends, — to produce conditions that would abolish crime, — and so unselfishly working for the elimination of his own profession. To me it seems just as certain that if the true physician must treat the whole man, if he is to cure physical ailments, so moral obliquities demand the same treatment of the true lawyer. That disease leads to sin and crime is quite as true as that sin and crime lead to disease. A man in the full flush of health and in good surroundings is less likely to become a criminal than a weakling in a bad environment.

One of our first pieces of work among the fishermen was to oust the floating grogshops

from the fishing fleet, by supplying vessels
in their midst which made provision for all
their legitimate demands: such as cheap
tobacco, social opportunities, and simple
religious teaching, but not alcoholic liquors.
This policy so commended itself to the
magistrates of the fishing seaports, that
we hold their written and unasked testi-
monials to the lessening of crime and even
the reduction of police forces in the fishermen's quarters, and the diminution of
poverty and the need of poor-relief. Eventually the results seemed so desirable to
conservative governments bordering the
German Ocean that they agreed to an international convention. It favored and
enforced the most severe laws against sell-
ing any liquors on the high seas, on the sole
ground that if their environment was improved, the lives of the people would also
be improved, a deduction fully indorsed by
the results founded on the experimental,
the best of all bases. The same principle
obtained on the shore when we supplied

institutes belonging to the fishermen, and had laws passed to prevent wages being paid in saloons or annexes thereto. The same results accrued in Labrador and North Newfoundland when the sale of liquor was prohibited in a region where such a law could be enforced. The aged mayor of Portland, Maine, near the close of a most successful business career, told me that though the liquor traffic, almost all-powerful, had done its best to make the prohibition laws ineffective, and to falsify their results, crime had unquestionably been lessened.

The absence of the environment of the open saloon and flaunting windows, and the nameless crimes connected with that traffic, are alike dependent largely on the prevention of the sale of intoxicants. The celebrated Judge Altgeld, when governor of Illinois, stated pithily that ninety-five per cent of crimes of violence and burglary were due to the same cause (alcohol). To my mind part of the privilege of the lifework of the Christian lawyer is to help to improve the environment of the tempted classes. To see justice impartially administered is of course his supreme special function; and there again he has the same opportunities as the doctor for the real joys of personal service to the oppressed, and for righting the wrongs of the injured. But would any worthy member of the bar contend that therewith ended the function of the true lawyer; that to exact retribution, to deter evildoers by threats, or even to get justice for those in trouble, made a great lawyer? Such a course might make him a rich lawyer, a popular lawyer, but would not make him great. To render crime unattractive, to implant new aspirations, to regenerate the individual, and to make laws remedial, are surely truer claims to immortality.

The laws have been framed by the powerful of a generation gone, and naturally leave us a heritage that demands remodeling if it is to meet the needs of a new era.

Why should men hesitate to apply the same test to the dogmas of the churches, which are the outgrowths of despotism, and not applicable to a true democracy as are its teachings? A real human sympathy with the life of to-day shows that there is infinite opportunity for simplifying the processes of the law, if it is to express our views of Christ's ideal of brotherhood, or even to give the poor man a chance of getting justice or to make the rich man fear punishment.

While working eight years in the purlieus of Whitechapel, I learned beyond all question, first, that often all the punishments invented by the law and all the provisions made for the protection of life and property failed in many cases; and further, I saw, as I have seen since that time, that the very men whom the punishments only made worse were perfectly capable of reformation. Intelligent sympathy and practical love cure individuals who have been pronounced incurable — the very methods the Master advocated and calls for still. Among such translations of love is the administration of the new kind of prisons, such as that of the Massachusetts Reformatory. Here men are not punished again and again in prison for little or big breaches of discipline, but are simply helped not to fail by offering them temptations to be good and by rewards for success in the attempt. Thus, instead of insane isolation and brutalization, making men revengeful and despairing, interesting and remunerative industries are taught and work is demanded, — good solid work, a temptation many criminals never get outside, and a gain, as they never had a chance to learn any craft before. More important still, good work is immediately made remunerative. Decorations, such as good conduct stripes, are displayed on the uniforms, and each new one means a shortened sentence. Responsibility and trust are gradually given them, and self-respect, hope, and aspiration induced and encouraged; pride and even *esprit de corps* are cultivated, — though as yet there are no inter-reformatory athletic contests, so far as I know!

There are plenty of people, however, who still maintain "once a criminal, always a criminal." There are many ever ready to condemn to the pathologically incurable class, those who often enough are only the victims of circumstance. The Master never was among these critics. He was ever the world's apostle of optimism and of hope. The amazing records of this Reformatory show that seventy-five per cent of these poor fellows are cured; of the remainder, fifteen per cent being physical degenerates. I say poor fellows, for my view is that they are to be pitied, if only because of the hell on earth which they make for themselves, and the loss of capacity and the vision of what God intended them to be. But unless we have a vision ourselves of the true greatness of our opportunity, we can hardly expect to sympathize with them for their blindness.

It is not the intellectual faculties to which Christianity seeks to supply new *information*, but it is the heart that it is necessary to reach. The Master always taught that the renewal and perfecting of a man was dependent upon a new heart, and no one has improved on that treatment that I know of. The efforts of the conventional, perfunctory religious teacher, like those of the sloppy and shallow pietist, remind me strongly of such drugs as tartarated antimony. If rightly given, the desired result is obtained, but if wrongly, it is promptly rejected. It is not religiosity or intellectualism, but love, that is needed. I claim that the great lawyer will be as eager as any specialist in talking, to translate wisely, into permanent effective methods for reclamation, the true religion, namely, the love that saves.

Dr. Richard Cabot and others in medicine, Dr. Elwood Worcester and other clergy, have accepted and eloquently taught by example and precept the necessity and the privilege in their two professions of considering causally and remedially the family and the immediate home surroundings of those they are endeavoring to help. Of course a great deal of a lawyer's work does not permit any such opportunity, yet I feel that the Master himself as a lawyer to-day would find chances to exercise the same spirit. Ætiology and pathology, sociology and theology, have found a parallel in the study of criminology which is evidence of the opening of fresh and glorious channels for life energies in the sister profession of the law. So young is it, however, that the Italian Lombroso, who is considered the parent of it, is still living in Italy. Germany has developed the study, and Professor Wigmore of Chicago is responsible for a society and a journal of criminology of Illinois.

In the amusing comic opera, the "Mikado," a verse of song runs: —

"My object all sublime
I shall achieve in time,

To make the punishment fit the crime,
The punishment fit the crime."

Yet what an ideal service, what a real success and joy the universal accomplishment or even serious effort toward its fulfillment would be, working in the Master's spirit of love for the man and hatred for the sin. That would imply that success in the effort spelled new men out of old, though science and evolution call the criminals hopeless. The real object of the lawyer's life can be attained only by offering his quota, infinitesimal though it be; but he can contribute it by reincarnating the spirit of the Master.

I would inquire here in what possible way the achievement of this glorious and ultimate end can be materially influenced by the lawyer's mere mental apprehension of or submission to subtle theologic dogmas or refinements in the precise method of expressing his devotion to God. What connection have such things, *per se*, with real religion? They may help his religion, but

they are not it. Plain, common courage
has much more influence than intellectual
attitude. Heney, who in the face of almost
every pessimist on earth, in the face of ap-
palling difficulties and opposition, in the
face of persecution and attempted murder,
sent the great civic burglars in San Fran-
cisco to jail, preached a gospel in the true
spirit of the Christ. For a poor Carpenter
to stand alone before the powers that be,
knowing that no protection was afforded
life by the law of his day, and say publicly,
"You generation of vipers! How can you
escape the damnation of hell?" required
courage, not theology. The cross of Christ
calls for intelligent courage and not intellectual effacement and mere ability to swallow. When Heney went back after scarcely
recovering from his wounds, and faced the
court, and again, after two mistrials, com-
menced a third, he, a volunteer, unpaid
in dollars, fighting almost as a lone man
against the immeasurable burden of hatred
and opposition, to me presented at least

one aspect of the truly great Christian
lawyer.

What is a corporation lawyer to do, you
say, when possibly his very living depends
upon his winning a technicality for the
bosses against equity for the community.
Abraham Lincoln would not take cases
when he knew his side was in the wrong,
and that winning meant doing a wrong.
To connive at the defeat of justice is to
prostitute a holy duty. That's all; you
must be brave if you are to have courage.
You must take adverse chances if you are
to be a hero. It is simply a question of
what you seek in life. The purely imper-
sonal position of the lawyer of course is the
easiest path, exactly as it is for the doctor
who asks, as Cabot says, "What is in the
waiting-room? Anything of interest?" I
acknowledge that to sympathize with each
case is difficult; it makes a claim on a lawyer which must curtail his practice. But he
is doing what he would like done for him
were he the client. And I am contending

that it is possible, and constitutes the true scale by which to measure greatness, and is what the Master would give, and what faith in him calls for.

Although owing to lack of time I have been unable to touch upon the three types of mind into which it would appear one might divide men, — the scientific, the literary, and the practical, — still I maintain that one principle applies to all. "But Jesus does not classify people. He gathers up the different types of human life into one comprehensive unity of discipleship." [1] In discussing the doctor and the lawyer I believe that I have in substance demonstrated the working-out of the Christian ideal, whatever the category into which a man may fall. "There is no activity of man which may not be the door, and into which and through which cannot enter that power of God which makes the man indeed to be God's servant." [2]

[1] Paradise, *The Church and the Individual.*
[2] Phillips Brooks.

LECTURE III

"GRANTED the reality of religion, what is its contribution to modern life?" I have already warned you that my idea in these lectures is to defend the rationality and value of faith in Christ on the basis of my own physical, mental, and spiritual experiences. I do not pretend that I possess scientific acquaintance with our peculiar social conditions, nor do I claim to have any special expert knowledge of the most successful ways of improving them. The world is just learning that the first can only be gained by the same patient study we devote to medicine or law; the second, I am certain, only by a life of personal devotion.

It is necessary to do, not merely to talk, if we are to know the truth about the remedies for life's troubles and difficulties. Still, with Browning, I realize that "God must be gained by first leap," and the object of this lecture is not to show that by any intellectual process man by searching can demonstrate God, but only that, with the advance of civilization, there is not a less but an ever-increasing need for what real religion has to contribute. There is proof enough of this on every hand for the man who is willing to experiment, to justify to his own mind his taking that leap, for society's benefit if not for his own.

One thing more is necessary to be made clear before going further, and that is, what do we mean by religion? By religion, in this lecture, I mean that following of the Christ which is a daily endeavor to interpret his teachings by translating them into action; or, in other words, trying to do what he would do if he were in our circumstances. If you were a housemaid, that would require you, in the words of the Salvation Army hymn, "to dust the shelf behind the door"; or if you were a king, "just to

king well," as one of your own humorists
suggests.

Jesus was peculiar among religious teachers in being "no mere speculative philosopher," no pure scientist for science'
sake. He was not of the type of Holmes's
Scarabee. I always think of him as the
family physician of the human race. Religion to him existed for the purpose of
action; it was valuable solely for the service of mankind. In the very simplest
language he tells us, not what God would
have us think, but what God would have
us do; putting within the reach of our daily
life that which not only spells our redemption here and now, but also enables us
to be redeemers ourselves, and so allows
us to contribute that which is lasting to
modern life. Was it not exactly in this
faith that these lectures were founded?

Yet religion in the past has spent far
more time and energy, and endured far
more suffering and sacrifice and defeat, in
endeavoring to perpetuate crystallized intel-

lectual attitudes and man-devised organ-
izations, all calling themselves "churches,"
than in trying to reincarnate the life of the
Master in their own.

A few years ago the visible churches
awoke to the fact that they were fast becoming what is known as "back numbers";
and that the profession of the minister of
religion was in danger of being side-tracked.
They are awake now, however, and on
all sides they are offering an increasingly
valuable quota to modern civilization.
"Churches" to me comprise all those religious institutions which, through helping
forward the reign of truth, mercy, and
reverence, induce righteousness, joy, and
peace, which is the Kingdom of God. Christ
himself says that their labels do not count
for anything. The way we salute our general is of much less importance than the
way we obey him. Victory is more momen-
tous than tactics. "Christian men," to
the Master, were those who were on his
side, and every such institution, whether

Protestant or Catholic, Jewish or purely ethical, is directly enriching our life to-day. Nor is "the state merely a local association existing to prevent mutual injury and promote universal exchange. . . . The object of the political association is not merely a common life, but noble action," says Aristotle.[1]

The churches are awaking to the fact that the state can and must be "religious"; and that just in proportion as an institution has no creed, its religion can be universal. Christ himself propounded no creed, and all the churches can unite on those lines which call for no special creed, but merely for the recognition of man's brotherhood, which each and every church acknowledges. In this way we see the great hope of their future in the federation of churches which is everywhere growing up, and which is striving to unite all their efforts for the betterment of social conditions.

Let us take now, as instances, some of the

[1] Dr. Lyman Abbott, *Yale Lectures*.

outgrowths of the churches. I myself have
seen enough of the Young Men's Christian
Association and Young Women's Christian
Association to know that, with their
splendid buildings and intelligent work,
they are materially adding to the comfort
and uplift of life of tens of thousands, nay,
of thousands of thousands, not only in this
country, but the whole world round. They
have even tried to make war comfortable.
Apparently it narrows the limits of agencies
to have to give examples and to name any
particular helpful factors; but a doctor is
impelled to illustrate his principles by
quoting cases. Thus, again, who that
knows anything of Robert College and its
work, which helped so much to give freedom to Turkey; of the Beyrout College
and its magnificent work for Syria and for
the Mohammedan world generally; of the
colleges in India which have shown that,
given a chance, the downtrodden classes
can successfully compete with the highest
castes; of the huge hospitals in China, Ja-

pan, India, and the Islands of the Sea, —
but knows perfectly well the truth that the
churches are contributing liberally. To the
nations everywhere Christianity is teaching the real value of human life, and so,
especially in the East, is raising the whole
aspiration of the people by making them
understand what they may become. This
is so much the case that in Japan the
wisest scholars have declared that only
in Christianity can they see an adequate
basis for individual and national life. They
make this statement in spite of the facts
of the liquor and opium traffic carried on by
Christian nations; in spite of anti-Christian
travelers, bad officials, the selfishness of
so-called governments, and the fallibility
of missionaries and their methods.

To-day there is so much prejudice against
the title "missionary" that many people,
apparently, prefer to consider their lives
purposeless rather than to admit that
"mission" is only a synonym for "life."
We must remember that there are many

failures in American social life, and yet
here also are many lives which are effective contributions to the world's economy.
I do not wish to weary you with examples,
but my interests being among sailors I
might here testify to the value of such
splendid institutes as that of your American Seaman's Society, recently erected in
New York; to the similarly efficient but less
expensive plants here in Boston, and to institutions of the same kind scattered all
round the world. These all give men who
are away from their homes a warm welcome,
a place to rest and play, a good cheap lodg-
ing, and a safeguard from the land-shark
and the crimp. Through all of these religion is making a serious Christian effort
towards the solution of a problem which
menaces the domestic life of those whose
life-service to the community necessarily
deprives them of the natural protection
and help of their own homes. To me this
is simply paying a debt to those to whom
the cost of catching our fish and transport-

ing our merchandise is often only to be
reckoned in "lives of men." It is still the
privilege of religion to see that this debt is
paid. If she fails to do so, some day it will
be recognized by the men themselves as
their right, and their own unions will provide it, once more taking from the church
a chance to justify herself. Nay, more, this
will anyhow be just as surely the case, if
into the church's interpretation of religion she introduces the sense of patronage
and intellectual superiority which have
characterized her too much in the past, and
which so ill become her as a servant of the
Master.

There are more instances than one of
big plants of this kind, just suited for practical messages of love, being totally unsuc-
cessful because their flavor is spoiled by a
sense of the "holier-than-thou" arrogance.
It is this fact that makes men say that these
efforts do little more than touch the real
problem. Believe me, it is sadly enough
that the working man passes the building

which *promises* exactly what he needs. If
he does not enter, it is because he feels that
the building is not really his. *Per contra*,
an eminently successful effort of this kind
to meet the needs of the working men is
Hollywood Inn at Yonkers, New York. It
was created by an Episcopal clergyman,[1]
but is owned and run by the men themselves. They and their unions all find a home
there, as do their clubs, their societies, and
their friends. It is theirs. There they play
what games they like. It just stands for
clean games without gambling, and for
drinks without alcohol. No public worship
or preaching is considered necessary. It
is just a demonstration of love, not a verbal
message. As a result of it, Mr. Freeman's
church found a thousand new commun-
icant members, because he preached the
undeniable Gospel.

Ten thousand other practical agencies
are ever more and more trying to do things

[1] Rev. James Freeman, now of St. Mark's Church,
Minneapolis.

in Christ's spirit, and these are forcing the world to acknowledge the contribution to life which religion can make. The increasing number of thoughtful men pouring out of our colleges, anxious to give life and intellect and money to the service of the world, is itself an offering which no man can estimate — though any fool can sneer at it. The growing passion for service has helped as many to work at home as it has sent out for that purpose to foreign fields.

To all intents and purposes, the *old idea* of the church is dying, if not dead. Thank God if it is. I could say with a whole heart, "The Church is dead! Long live the Church!"

But while it is good to review what the churches have accomplished, and to be able to derive from that courage and zeal for more service, the fact that there has been some success must be used only to prove to us that we can, and therefore *must*, do more. It is from the lips and pens of acknowledged leaders of many churches, and from those who have given the most earnest thought to the subject, that we learn that, so far as some of the most vital issues of modern life are concerned, the visible churches at the present time are practically a side issue. Most assuredly their future existence depends upon the attitude which they now adopt. Other agencies outside all the communions will, if *they* fall short, take out of their hands the only functions which they can find to occupy their energies.

Thus, for example, at one time the church afforded all the educational advantages. At the bar of public opinion she was found guilty of prostituting that sacred office for purely party purposes, and so she has forfeited her right to the performance of that most vital function.

Social settlement workers, civic leagues, rightly administered labor unions are advancing ends which righteousness demands, and which the churches have considered "outside their province." As if they could afford to be silent, or sit on the fence, when any question affecting the vital issues of life was concerned. Only the other day here in Boston, in a book shop, I overheard two clergymen talking of the efforts made by the charity organization in their town to cope with the "social evil." They had evidently been asked to coöperate, and one minister was explaining his refusal to the other by the remark, "But of course that sort of thing is quite outside the church's domain."

The man who is going to advance the Kingdom of God in the world in any way must be in the world enough to understand it. A clergyman whom I know always dresses in a light business suit and invariably lunches at a down-town club, that he may mix with other men, as the Galilean Carpenter did, and so may know the real minds and interests of those he is trying to help. Only by understanding a patient's needs can any physician hope for success.

It is no use merely shouting, "Down with rich corporations," however bad they may be, unless we are prepared to find substitutes for them. Christ's religion especially is bound to be constructive. There is a danger of the shallow man shouting that his voice may be heard, just as there is that the scholar may be led into thinking too much. The proof of this is not difficult to discover. We have only to go and see why it is that some preachers face empty pews while other churches are packed with men.

The people in these days gauge things by their practical value; and men go to the church only if it has something to give them. They will go to " divine service" only if they find it inspires them to express better their own devotion in human service. This fact has further been exemplified among our own fishermen by a fishermen's union which started twelve months ago, and now has seventeen thousand members. In another twelve months it promises to include the whole number of the most virile among them, because it has already helped them to get a fairer return for their labor, and to make their own voices heard in matters which concern their direct home and personal interests.

In our country the church buildings are more ornate and comfortable than ever,— better auditoriums, better heated, aired, and seated. The clergy are adding lantern lectures, social gatherings, and all the latest attractions copied from the churches here. But in spite of all this the pews are actually not one whit more crowded than when I went there twenty years ago.

The fact is that as yet church members have not realized the acuteness of the social problem. In Labrador this is excusable. There we are still living in a period of a hundred years ago. Our laboring classes have not yet acquired the advantages of education. They have only just begun to discover that if the workers go hungry and naked, while the thinkers live in super-

tion which they have occupied in men's estimation, and which they still occupy, was fully justified, and will, I believe, be more and more deeply realized, whatever happens in the future to dogmatic theology. Their attractiveness was undoubted, for everywhere men joined them; not for what they could get, for that was seldom attractive, but for what they could in their turn give. It certainly was not so much the desire for gain here or hereafter, as the belief that the Kingdom of God on earth could use what they had to contribute, that fired men's hearts to loyalty for the organization they founded. The mistaken idea of the immediate coming of the end of the world and the short road to eternal bliss was no doubt a comfort and an attraction to them. But it was not their Master's teaching as we read it. It is evidence of the continued human liability to error even among those who were the very closest to Christ's person. When men were near to Christ, they needed nothing but the atmosphere of his spirit to attract them to him, but as they got farther and farther away from him in spirit and in time, they used this doctrine as a bait to compensate for the loss involved in this world by becoming his followers. But I will not believe it was ever the chief factor in the appeal to follow Christ, any more than the promise attached to the Fifth Commandment makes me honor my father and mother.

As for the name "Christian," it was originally given in contempt, and was used by men of the world as a stigma and a reproach. From that reproach Christians themselves soon redeemed it by displaying the spirit of Christ. It came to stand for that humility, mercy, and justice which the Scripture tells us God calls for still. It spelled loyalty, courage, and self-sacrifice; and the world, ever able to recognize if not always willing to accept the noblest, in a few centuries changed its attitude. The Christian knight became the ideal of history.

It was not long, however, before the organization of the scattered groups into bodies for mutual strength and protection began seriously to disturb the minds, not only of those who represented the vast interests of religion, but of the temporal powers as well. Rich as well as poor began to feel the force of the call of Jesus, and he found followers even in Cæsar's household. The simplicity and attractiveness of the Christian was a protest against evil. How is it we seldom see any persecutions of modern Christians? It is certainly not because there is no graft in high places.

When for the first time I wandered through the old Coliseum at Rome, it was at night, by moonlight, and the spirits of the men who had suffered upon the very ground I trod seemed almost visible. I, a so-called Christian, felt humiliated, not repelled.

Yet persecution never really injured the growth of faith in Christ. Those who tried to follow in his footsteps grew more and more numerous. Rottenness began from within. In the organization itself there grew up rank and privilege; talkers began to count as higher than workers and claim for themselves special proximity to the Master. As if Jesus himself had not talked far more in works than in words, had not laid far more emphasis on works, had not devoted far more time to works, and had not referred those in doubt to his works as his indorsement. This restraint on Christ's part from laying down dogmas is more remarkable, the longer one thinks about it. That sects should still be unable to settle whether Saturday or Sunday is the true day of rest, that men should be able even to attempt to defend slavery, or to try to enforce celibacy on the authority of his teaching, is evidence of the scope he left for individuality by never laying down minute rules, but only enunciating general principles.

Yet it is always easier to talk than to do, and presumably the cleverer men soon discovered this. Alas, talking, more especially on matters or facts about which we cannot appeal to our physical senses, is just as likely to divide as doing is certain to unite. As late as the Reformation, no theological question was too slight to engender hatred, and even to provoke civil war. Indeed, so began the differences which invented "heresy," and then councils and creeds to define and locate and eradicate it.

With the advent of classes in the church, one ruling and the other serving, social differences became easy to justify, and in fact almost inevitable. Moreover, it seemed suddenly to dawn on the real outsiders, the men without the Master's spirit, that Christianity was a mighty force, and formed a bond between men which was far more durable than any involuntary one. It only needed careful using and it would serve to bolster up temporal as well as spiritual power. So gradually was evolved the complex and immense structure of the Papacy. Eventually there followed in the name of Christ so fantastic an interpretation of his service as the Crusades. Whatever the church taught verbally, it practically set up at that period the possession of property as an object for worship, and so at once destroyed the Christ vision of the paramount value of life.

Like the graphic representation of the human heart beat on the sphygmographic drum, the track of real Christ-following through history seems to have risen and fallen in a kind of rhythm, though at times, like a hectic temperature chart, to have been little above the neutral line. Whether there will ever be millennial peace on earth, or whether the waxing and waning warfare is essential for the evolution of our souls' welfare, may be open to question, but that the true Christ-following has always brought out the heroic in men is not open to doubt. It seems somehow that conflict is necessary for the perfection of character. I know that in navigating our coast to-day I feel twice as reliable a pilot for the bad times I have had on so many rocks.

Anyhow, the organization designed to foster and safeguard Christ's Kingdom gradually deprived men of all personal freedom. The leaders not only "suffered themselves to be called Master," but positively liked it, and eventually insisted they were so, till the persecutions which they themselves instituted against men who evinced Christ's spirit were ten times more cruel than those instigated by the early pagans. The Duke of Alva was a type of such men. But in spite of this, the organization harbored all the while the living germ, without which it must have died, and with which, with all its shortcomings, it slowly helped to advance the true Kingdom of God. The germ, however, sometimes sank to the bottom, like the currants in a badly mixed cake, and few managed to obtain it.

The biographies and autobiographies of men of action have always been the most

attractive literature to me. Whether or
not they have had the orthodox label, the
appeal of such lives is just as great and
must tend to kindle any spark of manliness
in us — that our brief day of life may also
be used to some noble purpose. To me it
has been a thousand times helpful to look
back upon the story of the centuries, and
realize how differently men interpret the
call of God to them, and how varied are
the services which can be approved as
"Christian." It is only the brave efforts
through the ages of men of that type, men
often of very ordinary attainments, which
have even partially given us back our freedom to-day. But we are still far from spirit-
ually free. Numbers of men and women
are still tangled up in the meshes and intri-
cacies of theologies and theories and con-
ventions. Many are still satisfied to sub-
mit to external authority instead of their
individual vision. But if religion is to
grapple with the social questions of to-day,
to attract when it can no longer compel,

and to satisfy the practical minds of modern youth, it must come down from heaven to earth, and this even though the process will involve much heart-burning on the part of the theologian, and still some martyrdom on the side of those who break with the old order.

How are men to decide who is a Christian or how far the inability to say, "Rabbi, thou art the Christ, the Son of God," made eleven out of twelve disciples forfeit their right to the title? For example, no body of men will agree as to the claims of world-influencing writers like Goethe, Shakespeare, or Locke; of scientists who have advanced knowledge, like Copernicus, Newton, or Darwin; of artists who have altered the conception of art, like Raphael, Michael Angelo, or Da Vinci; of statesmen who have changed the course of history, like William of Orange or Oliver Cromwell; of earnest truth-seeking philosophers so different as Plato, Kant, and Spencer; indeed, any of the whole gamut of human

beings whose lives have been used for the
amelioration of the conditions of life on
earth, and have contributed their quota
toward making the Kingdom of God more
possible here and now. We are too apt to
grudge other people their haloes, and too
fond of trying to preen our own — a difficult matter under any circumstances! Our
judgment ought surely to depend upon
what we consider *was* the Kingdom Christ
came on earth to found. The Kingdom
of God for which I am working is an ideal
world, a world in which the soul's environment, which of course includes the body
in which it dwells, must be made more ideal.
Even pagans so long ago as the philosopher
Lucian stated the opinion that the soul is
as much helped by the flesh as the flesh by
the soul. Yet it has become necessary for
both of these truths to be demonstrated
alongside us in Boston, as if they were new
discoveries of the twentieth century. They
seem to have been forgotten or neglected
by the churches.

That is exactly what gives us the fun of service — because it includes everything we can do to help out. The "joy of service" is so much exalted in these days that one might almost suppose there existed normally a craving for the joy of uselessness. That is the supreme joy of the barnacle, who, though born a free-swimming animal, prefers even in his youth a life of inaction, and after fastening his head to a rock spends the remainder of his days kicking food into his mouth with his hind legs.

Again, surely we can look upon as disciples of the Christ all those who from purely patriotic motives have devoted their stay on earth to the welfare of their country, and at personal risk and sacrifice have sought to raise her to their highest ideals. Fighting may not be the ideal Christian way to gain an end, but we must remember that Christ does not judge men by what they do not see, but by what they do see. Who would not gladly face the supreme tribunal, so far as their patriotism is concerned, with the record of Gustavus Adolphus, Joan of Arc, Count Cavour, Louis Kossuth, the Duke of Wellington, or George Washington, and among living men the heroes of the Japanese War? Or, seeing the cruel straits and horrible conditions inflicted on Germany by Napoleon, who would not follow a Stein, a Bismarck, or a Moltke? Certainly many of these men think *themselves* Christians just as much as we regard *ourselves* in that light. I was reared on stories like that of General Havelock and his saints, of Clive and Lawrence, of Wolfe and Drake. It will probably be long, however, before the French believe Bismarck was not lying when he said: "If I did not believe Providence had destined this nation for something great and good, I should at once give up my position as a diplomat or never have entered on it at all." Yet human judgment on a Gordon who stayed the cruelties of the Taiping Rebellion, or a Cromwell who opposed the divine right of kings, or even a Lincoln who fought to free his fellows from slavery will no doubt be different according to the tribunal before which they are tried. The right interpretation of true loyalty must be left to each man's conscience. Moses, David, and Paul expressed their willingness to be castaways themselves if their people might be saved. For my part, I can quite conceive the profession of arms, at any rate in the past, as being a religious service, and as often seeming to such men the only means available for advancing the Kingdom of God. Centurions were among Christ's first followers. Personally, I thank God for the view of a wide and ever-changing range of service.

The unendurable miseries of the masses at the time of the French Revolution called for a Christian champion and found none. Surely this was only for lack of the vision of their opportunities. Even if the churches of any day are no more Christian than the temporal powers, nevertheless, God's purposes will be wrought out without us if we will not help. There can be no doubt that the ultimate result of the Revolution was a distinct gain to the kingdom of righteousness, joy, and peace, — that the present happy and prosperous French peasantry was made possible by it, and that the lessons it impressed on the rulers of the world materially hastened the broader brotherhood of man. But had true men with the Master's spirit been forthcoming to guide the process, who can doubt but that the same ends could have been accomplished without the horrors and infamies that the Revolution involved? It was Guizot, not an ecclesiastic, who, when he fled to England as the only stable throne in Europe, said to Lord Shaftesbury, "Sir, it is their religion which has saved the English nation."

It sometimes takes catastrophes to show the church as well as the world the incalculable opportunities to make life worth while, which they are constantly throwing away. That it is as much the vision as the will which men need is shown by the fact that only five years before the Revolution a French historical philosopher wrote: "The political system of Europe has arrived at perfection. Few reforms are needed. There is no need nowadays to fear a revolution." [1]

As an absolute antithesis to the services of the physical fighter to the Kingdom of God, take that of the philosopher, Hugo Grotius. Stirred by the wholesale condemnation of people to death for heresy, and the frightful cruelties perpetrated on the innocent and noncombatants in war, he satisfied his passion for service by the writing of long books in Latin. By his immortal work, "De Jure Belli et Pacis," he awakened the world to the Christian sense of God's international family, and he laid the foundation for all future international law. There seems no fear of the

[1] *Seven Great Statesmen.*

overcrowding of this particular branch of service to-day; the writing of books in Latin is a little out of vogue. But who shall doubt that it was a truly Christian service, and that the law schools to-day have God-like opportunities yet open to them before the reign of peace universal.

It is not part of my scheme to publish a schedule of Christian services. In ten thousand experiences of everyday life we cannot fail to see that God not only permits but seeks our coöperation in the establishment of his Kingdom. If we find this out too late and have to look back on a life full of opportunities which we have let slip, we can have no longer any excuse to mitigate our remorse.

Now that we cannot be forced to do so, we no longer admit that God will only make his will plain through a third party. God certainly does make plain the way of life to those who seek it in sincerity and truth. We are no longer accountable to human authority. Bismarck once rebuked the autocratic Wilhelm the First for sneering at the word "pietist," by saying, "Christianity is not the creed of Court chaplains." And the finicking arguments of the religionists made the great Doctor Jowett of Balliol, Oxford, once say, "All wise men have the same religion, but no wise man will say what it is."

It will surely comfort some who, from their evangelical point of view, might be troubled with fears that this broad interpretation was dangerously modern and incompatible with the simple teaching of the Gospel, to know that so unquestionable a Christian as George Fox taught that "every hunger of the heart, every dissatisfaction with self, every sense of shortcoming, shows that the soul is not unvisited by the Divine Spirit. To want God at all implies some acquaintance with Him." In all sorts and conditions of men Fox always appealed to "that of God," or "the Christ within them." We know them by their fruits, not by their catechisms.

The only real heathen and heretics are the purely selfish. It is for our own sakes as well as theirs that we desire their conversion. For while they are losing all life has to give, we are losing the share they might contribute. Alas, there are still many rich in talents who find it costs too much simply to follow the Master.

For my part, I am so sure that God is Love that I never worry a moment about whether divine wisdom and power could n't have devised an easier road for redemption than willing personal service. That to me is simply loyalty, and of that quality the *professing* Christian has no monopoly.

I never believed that following the Master meant having no will of our own. Christ had a will of his own. We are "to stand on our feet, and hear what the Lord will say to us." God wants men with a will. Only that will must be linked with God's. Self-will and selfishness are always obviously an absolute bar to unity between God and man and between man and man. I have always had a holy horror of the teaching that the Christian religion calls for a backboneless type of person, the simpering, long-haired, effeminate creature so familiar in "sacred art."

Art is no art at all if it is n't sacred, if it does n't comfort and uplift. It does n't inspire me to see my ideal of human life, the Christian knight, the man of every age and every station and every calling who is doing God's work, held up to ridicule as a sickly, effeminate imbecile. I always pictured the Christ at college as captain of the football team, or stroke of the 'Varsity boat, or one of the honor men, because these were what I wanted to be myself.

It is this hideous teaching, that secular and sacred can be separated, and must be labelled so, which formerly made men estimate the claimants to religion at their own valuation: namely, that they were fitted for talking, but not for competing in anything else which pertains to human life, and were chiefly remarkable for the things they did not do. "Consecration, not renunciation, makes the highest character." [1]

So long as we make the division, so long as Christ-following does not mean every single method and way that can make this world better and brighter, Christ-following is robbed of its dignity, its joy, its utility, — and its future.

Let us descend to the concrete for a moment. In Labrador it was religious to conduct public worship, to lead a prayer-meeting, to marry, to baptize, to bury, to take up collections, to foster guilds. It was secular to do medical, legal, commercial, or any kind of work by which men can earn a living. It was religious to visit and condole with the hungry. It was very distinctly secular to run a coöperative store and feed them. It was religious to pray on Wednesday night that God would give the people a good fishery. It was secular on Thursday to make twine cheap, to build a bait freezer, and to introduce motor dories.

[1] Doctor Allen.

It was religious to give old clothing to naked families. It was secular to introduce looms, sheep, reindeer, and to teach the women to weave durable and fitting woolen clothing for their families. It was religious to pray that God would keep idle folk's hands from mischief. It was secular to set to work to keep those same hands remuneratively busy. Finally, in Labrador, none but "fossil men" wondered why every one wanted to be "worldly." If Christ's men are to be known by their works, surely Christ's work is to be known by its efficiency to redeem.

I have spent now much of your time and mine in defending the perfect rationality of Christian faith. I have suggested many times that like all other things it must be accepted or rejected on the ground of its practical value. But I realize that it is as a surgeon that I am addressing you. I would naturally expect you to ask now, "What are the specific things which I can do to gain the faith which you consider so valuable?"

If I am right and you are looking to these

lectures for such advice as I may have to give here and now from my own experience, I should say first of all cut out whatever sin you are conscious of. You will find it an immense help to let it be known on which side you are. It takes a lot of pluck to do that, but it makes a man of one. It is still true that " whosoever would save his life shall lose it," and it must often be at the cost of ambition and popularity that the door of the Kingdom of Heaven is opened.

If the certain deterioration of physical and mental capacities through dallying in the slightest degree with drink and vice does not deter men from indulging in them, at least if they will follow the Christ they will refrain for the sake of making the path of righteousness easier for others.

All through my lectures my attitude will have appeared as depreciative to the organized churches. Believe me, my criticisms are the wounds of a friend. I realize that the conditions in America to-day are not those of England twenty years ago. The church certainly is beginning to wake up. Its members are realizing that there is a loose screw, and are looking about to locate it. I believe to-day you will find in her that which is essential for your development, namely, constructive work which you can do. She will also give you the realization of spiritual fellowship between yourself and God, and between yourself and others who are in earnest about life, which it is her especial prerogative to afford, and of which she should allow no other interest to deprive her. Join her and help her. She, too, to-day is making for the uplift of humanity. She needs all you can give; and she certainly will give it back to you again with interest.

For my part, I find the world is good. It is a most reliable paymaster, whichever way you make your investment, and I am glad to be in it. Everything seems to have a purpose, and from that fact I deduce a purposer. The world seems reasonable, and therefore likely to end reasonably. The evo-

lution of love, the development of intellect,
the unceasing metabolism of the body, considered with the principle of the conserva-
tion of energy, always seemed to me to argue
against the annihilation of personality. But
after all, it is only a reasonable service in
this world, not omniscience, which is asked
of me. Some men hate the whole universe,
because they realize how brief the tenure of
the things they love in life is. But I am no
pessimist. Knowing that I only stay for a
time alongside of what I call my property,
I am still delighted with all I get, enjoying
immensely the use of it while I have it, and
believing, as Christ teaches, that so-called
death cannot rob me of spiritual friendships
and assets. If I count what I can contribute
to life, and not what I can get out of it, that
of itself makes it worth while. The gauge
is not what we have, but what we do with
what we have.

I am as sure that I am not my body as I
am that I am not my house. But for all that,
I know that I am I, and that I shall always

continue to be so is sufficiently probable
to satisfy me. Exactly what will befall me
hereafter has not yet entered into the heart
of man. Judging from popular ideas, very
far from it.

That men in this world are by no means
physically equally endowed, every doctor
knows, and every mother ought to know.
Christ never taught that they were. He
insisted only that we should recognize our
common brotherhood, not that we should
quarrel about being unequal. As for the
free-will controversy, Christ taught that
the only free men are those whom he sets
free from the slavery of self. Self-service
was the captivity from which he came to
set his people free.

To suppose that all men's intellectual
capacities are identical is absurd, and yet
with this premise in a world of utterly imperfect knowledge we play at the solution
of religious unity, as if, under the circumstances, it could ever be uniformity, either
in thought or in method of expression. There

must ever be endless permutations and combinations when it comes to intellectual apprehensions. So long as we cling to any humanly devised definitions, which we insist upon as articles of faith necessary to salvation, we shall inevitably insure discord for all time. Together with these initial differences, and with imperfect data, we must take into consideration the changes which new environments and new experiences make in the same individual. Thus for my own part I was once absolutely intolerant of all forms and ceremonies in public worship. Now I expect to value ever more and more beauty and orderliness in the expression of it.

At the time of my own decision, twenty-five years ago, the current version of the doctrine of evolution was a very new and staggering idea to every one. But my faith was never seriously troubled. Perhaps the fact that at that time I was deep in the study of anatomy and physiology showed me that the temple of man's soul was so marvelously adapted to the environment of a world like this, that I saw no reason why we should have expected, as Balfour has since suggested, that just because a similar form suited lower animals, some new design ought to have been devised for us. Further, evolutionists argued, not only that all improvements in physical conditions were attained by intellectual processes such as the Davy safety lamp, or Jenner's vaccine, merely fortuitous advances further fitting our race for survival, but also that every disinterested motive, every spiritual impulse was just one more device for the same end. I never could believe such good fruit could come from such unpromising trees. Anyhow, I did n't want to believe it, for the boys I was teaching at that time needed no encouragement to go and steal the jam, as I found more than once at our annual summer encampment.

Materialism has shot its bolt anyway, and of late the pendulum has swung the other way. The new knowledge of the periodic law, the divisibility of the atom, the possible identity and intermutability of what we used to consider elements, the hypothesis that all matter is only after all a form of electricity or motion, the discovery of radium and the suggestion of the possibility of perpetual motion, all show us that of all the ways in which we interpret Scripture, none can possibly be considered final. Orthodox Christianity has suffered a good deal from lack of humility, but our scientific friends have little to boast of in that direction.

Because no one has been able to comprehend the doctrine of the Atonement, or to compress the definition of it into words, I see no reason to reject it, or for me to be anxious for those who fail to accept it. Definitions and doctrines, anyhow, were never vital to my faith. The realization of a living Christ, with all that that implies, seems all that he expected of me. Just to live, "as seeing him who is invisible," is my one ideal which embraces all the lesser ideals of my life; to do in all circumstances what I think he would do in my place, not what he would have done in Judæa two thousand years ago. There was no temptation to waste golden hours over bridge-whist in those days.

The expression of my religion has to be practical to satisfy me, though I have no doubt whatever of the religion of those who are satisfied with mystical experiences alone. I quite realize that my faith is only faith. But I know that every one has to begin all knowledge with faith. My faith is only my base for action, as is every one's else. Moreover, it is the only possible base. The faith of exceedingly fallible senses is at the bottom of all actions. It is a marvel that we get on as well as we do, seeing that the evidence of our senses so frequently deceives us. In reality they afford us no road at all by which to arrive at truth.

To act on faith seems to me to be on surer ground, and I try to strengthen it by reading my Bible with common sense. I am

glad to believe that his faith gave Barti-
meus his eyesight, — especially for Barti-
meus' sake, — for the value to me to-day of
a single cure done nineteen hundred years
ago is problematical, unless it teaches me
how to repeat it. But I believe my faith not
only made me see, but what is more, I do
actually believe it has enabled me to help
others to their vision, both physically and
mentally.

But what is the use of all this talking! I
would not cross the road, much less come
all the way from Labrador, unless I felt
there was some desirable end which might
be reached thereby. The object of the Noble
Lectures, as I have said, seemed to me a
decidedly practical one, namely, to induce
in the minds of the hearers a keener desire
to stand in life for just those things that
Christ stood for, to beget a determination
to reincarnate his life, and so attain the
whole achievement of which ours is capable.

How far this effort has been successful
only God knows. I have worried you with

long lists of names of men and the long records of deductions from other lives than
mine, solely because it seemed to me that
the best way to advocate the adoption of
principles is to illustrate their effect in action. Moreover, it is only from the empirical standpoint that I, a physician from
the confines of civilization, venture to address you in this metropolis of all philo-
sophies. The knowledge of the immense
factor in public life which your universities
have become was an additional incentive,
emboldening me to accept the invitation
you extended.

I have seen the results of the change of
attitude of the exponents of Christ's religion from the controversial and tyrannical
methods of so many centuries back to the
brotherly methods of the Master; from
the failure of their attempts to be their
brother's keeper, to success in becoming
their brother's brother. And to-day, ten
times more than ever before, I am an op-
timist as to the future. In spite of the in-

crease of Dreadnoughts and superdreadnoughts, I seem to see a distinct moral progress in the relation of nations to one another, and in the new social movement opportunities and improvement in the relation of man to man. Experience has taught me what a blessing for the real ills of humanity this promises. Surely I may plead that it is as compelling a force to a physician, this desire to give to others the benefits of a remedy he has come to value so highly himself, as is any professional oath he may have taken to keep secret no treatment he uses for physical ailments. Posterity has nothing but blame for a Morton who tried to patent the discovery of ether for his own benefit.

If our eyes are only open for vision, in ten thousand daily experiences we cannot fail to see opportunities for what we can give. We shall see God himself, not waiting for us to be good, but seeking our coöperation just where we stand, in the establishment of his Kingdom. What could be more terrible than to have to look back upon a life of opportunities, as is that of each of you, all of which we had let slip!

This experience brings me here to-day to try to induce you to accept as your life axiom, not merely that God was once reincarnated in human life, as an emotional submission, but that as an everyday matter of fact Christ walks in our streets to-day, and can again prove his divinity to us beyond question if we will permit him, by living in our human lives. There is no life but the life which comes from him; to me, as I have said, the rest is merely existence. The reason that Christ came was that we might have life, here and now, and that we might have it more and more abundantly.

THE END